PAINT, BRUSH
and PALETTE

by Harvey Weiss

YOUNG SCOTT BOOKS • NEW YORK

ROUEN CATHEDRAL, WEST FACADE, SUNLIGHT, *Claude Monet*
National Gallery of Art, Washington, D. C., Chester Dale Collection

Table of Contents

PART ONE Experimenting With Color

Most beginning artists use color purely by intuition—in a hit-or-miss fashion. Sometimes the results are excellent; often they are not. Intuition will always be the most important ingredient in the artist's paint box. But it will be much more effective if accompanied by an understanding of what color is all about.

The first part of this book tries to give you this understanding. There are experiments and explanations that give you the basic facts about color and how to use it. The second part of the book explains various painting materials, art principles and ideas, and shows you how to use them in making pictures. Oil paints, water colors and pastels are described, and there are examples of paintings by many artists which show you the possibilities of each medium. There are also some step-by-step demonstrations of how paintings are made—all of which will help you to be a better artist and to make you feel more at home with paint, brush, and palette.

Materials

The easiest paints to experiment with are poster or tempera colors. These paints can be thinned with water, and your brushes can be washed in water. They are inexpensive and available in any stationery, art or ten-cent store. Buy a jar of each of the primary colors: blue, yellow, red, and also white and black. Get at least two soft, round water-color brushes— one small #5, and the other larger, #10. You can use almost

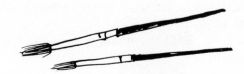

any kind of drawing paper, but make sure it is not too lightweight. A lightweight paper will buckle. It should be at least as heavy as the paper this book is printed on. You will also need two large jars of water, one to wash your brushes in each time you use another color, and one to hold clean water with which to thin your colors. You will need some sticks for stirring your paints in the jar, and three or four old dinner plates on which to mix your colors. It is also very helpful to have a drawing board. This is simply a large flat piece of wood on which you can thumbtack your paper. A piece of plywood 16 by 20 inches would be fine.

Getting Started – The Primary Colors

Red. Yellow. Blue. These are called primary colors in paint because we can use them to make the widest range of other colors. But in actual practice, you'll find that most artists buy quite a few additional colors such as browns and greens and violets, because it simplifies mixing. For a start, limit yourself to the three primary colors and black and white.

First stir your jars of red, yellow, and blue. If the color is too thick or is beginning to dry out, add a little water. The paints should have the consistency of heavy cream.

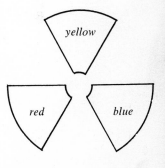

On a sheet of paper, paint a little square of each of your primary colors. Place the colors as shown in the drawing in the margin, and be sure to remember to wash your brush *thoroughly* before going from one color to the next.

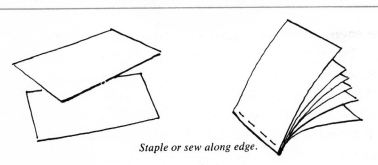

Staple or sew along edge.

It would be an excellent idea to make all of your color experiments on the same size sheet of paper—about 6 by 8 inches. Then you can sew or staple the pages together to make a "reference book" which you can look at from time to time when you are working on larger and more ambitious paintings.

The Secondary Colors

Put a couple of drops of yellow on one of your mixing plates. Wash your brush. Then add a couple of drops of blue. Mix these together and you have a secondary color: green. It is called a secondary color because it is made up of two primary colors. Paint a square of this green on your sheet of paper between the yellow and the blue.

Now mix yellow and red together and you have another secondary color: orange. Paint an orange square between the red and yellow. Then mix red and blue and put the purple you will get between the red and blue. You now have a color wheel which shows you all the primary and secondary colors.

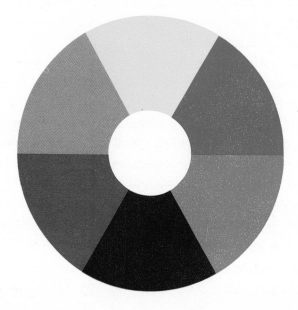

Complementary Colors

Any two colors directly opposite each other on the color wheel are called complementary. Complementary colors rarely look subtle or harmonious when placed together. A living room with blue walls and orange furniture would be a rather unrestful place to be in. (Blue and orange are complementary.) When you *mix* complementary colors you get dark greys and browns. If you mixed exactly equal amounts you would get black.

These two colors are complementary.

So are these.

Color Values

If you take a color—blue, for example—and add white to it, it is still blue, but of a lighter value. If you add black it is blue of a darker value. The "value" of a color is its lightness or darkness.

To see how color values change, try this little sequence of colors. Paint a square of pure blue in the center of a piece of paper. (If you are going to make a reference book, use the 6 by 8 inch size paper.) Mix some blue with just a little white

paint and put that to the right of the pure blue. Add more white to what you have and paint another square. Now start with white and add just a touch of blue, and put that on the end. Repeat the process, adding black instead of white to the blue, and place these colors to the left. When you finish you'll have one color, graded in value from very dark to very light.

Mixing Colors

Now that you know some of the vocabulary of color, let's begin to explore some more color possibilities. For example, using yellow as your basic color, see how many different kinds of yellow you can mix. Take a sheet of paper (your reference

Pure yellow and some of its variations.

book size) and start by painting a square of pure yellow in the center. Then add a touch of black to yellow. Paint a square of that color on your paper. Make up a little purple and see what happens when you add that to the yellow. See how many kinds of yellow you can make, and paint a square of each on your paper.

When you have exhausted the possibilities of yellow, take another two sheets of paper and do the same thing with your other two primary colors. This experiment shows you the enormous variety of colors that you can get using only the three primary colors and black and white.

When you are finished, ask yourself which color on each sheet of paper is the brightest or most intense. You'll find that it is always the pure primary color that you started with. The more colors you mix together the *less intense* your final mixture will be. "Intensity" is a word that is often used when talking about color. It refers to the purity and brightness of a color. Do not confuse "value" with "intensity." "Value" refers to how light or dark a color is. "Intensity" refers to how bright or pure it is.

Putting Color To Use

Now let's put all these colors to some use. First make a little painting using only *intense* colors. (Use a size paper that will fit into your reference book.) Keep your painting small and as

simple as possible, with only three or four elements—perhaps a tree, sky, a hill, and the sun. Use only your primary and secondary colors (yellow, blue, red, orange, green, purple) and use them at full intensity—not mixing them together nor adding white or black.

Your painting will certainly look very bright, and you will probably decide that there is too much intensity. It may look a little wild and garish. Stuart Davis, in his painting reproduced on Page 14, manages to use all these intense colors, but the mood and effect the artist wanted was one of violence and shrill nervousness.

Now see what happens when you paint exactly the same picture again, using colors that are *less intense*. Try adding a touch of white or black to some of the colors you are using. Use complementary colors mixed together, such as blue with orange, or purple with yellow. This second painting will be much more subdued and somber than the first one you made.

Warm Colors And Cool Colors

In addition to intense and subdued colors, there are two other kinds of color families: the warm colors and the cool colors. Look at the color wheel you made on Page 6. Which colors would you describe as warm in feeling? Red, yellow, orange, purple? These colors, as well as pink, mauve, rust, gold, and most browns, are warm colors. This kind of color suggests the sun, fire, bright hot days, the beach in July, a rocket blast, or an erupting volcano.

The cool colors of ice, shade, water, brisk winter days, mountain tops, and clear skys are blues and greens and variations of these.

Now paint the same little landscape two more times—first using only warm colors, then using the cool colors. Your painting with the warm colors will probably look like a hot August day. The picture painted with cool colors may come out like a chilly winter day.

Now line up your four little paintings and compare them. You will see how effectively color can convey a mood and feeling.

Combinations Of Colors

Any *single* color, by itself, looks attractive. Only *combinations* of colors can be harmonious or unpleasant, beautiful or ugly, dramatic or boring. There is no such thing as an ugly red, although there can be an ugly *combination* of red and another color.

Try some color groupings of the sort described here to see just how this works in actual practice. They will help you to familiarize yourself with colors in relation to one another and in various combinations.

With a pencil, rule off four squares in four places on a sheet of paper as illustrated in the margin. (Use the same size paper you used for your other experiments, so that you can include it in your reference book.) Fill in one of the squares in each group with your favorite primary color. Then try different colors in combination with it. If, for example, you've chosen red as your favorite color, in one group of squares try intense colors along with it—yellow, blue, green. In another group, try colors closely related to your red— perhaps pink, purple, red-brown. For the other groups, try to think of other color combinations that may be interesting. How would the red look with three cool colors? How would it look with various greys? How does it look with low-intensity colors, or with colors of a dark value?

Make as many groups of squares and try out as many different kinds of color combinations as you can think of. And as you mix and apply your colors, try to understand why some combinations are drab or clashing or ugly, and why others are harmonious or dramatic or pleasing.

The same kinds of choices that you make in these color experiments are made by the artist when he paints a picture. He is always asking himself what color (or shape or line) he should use to communicate best the mood or story or idea which is on his mind.

Here is a little experimental painting that uses only warm colors.

10

The blue in the upper right is the same in all these groupings. Here it is in competition with three other intense
colors to make a violent combination.

These colors are all cool. As a result, there is a rather
harmonious, peaceful feeling. There is a small amount of
blue in each of the colors.

Here we have a pure blue contrasting with three greys.
Because the blue is the most intense of the four it stands
out and dominates.

This is certainly a dreary and morbid combination of
colors. They are all of a rather dark value and without
much contrast of any sort.

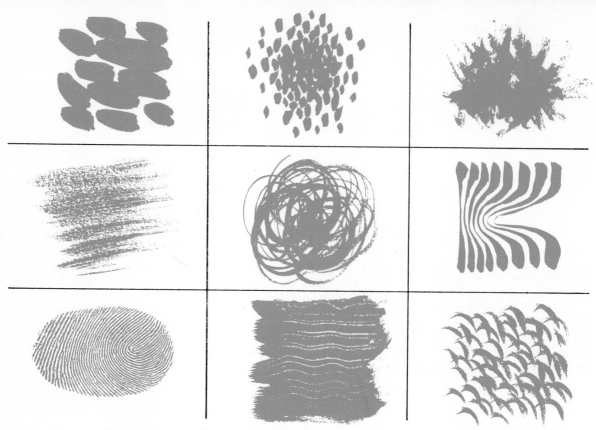

Textures

As you continue to work with color, you will find that its appearance is affected by the way it is applied to the paper. A color brushed on smooth and flat will look different from the same color brushed on thick and bumpy with quick rough brush strokes. These different paint surfaces are called "textures." They enable you to get variety in your paintings. Textures will also help you to suggest the feel of the objects you paint. For example, if you were painting a tree, you might apply the paint heavily, using short, choppy brush strokes to indicate the quality of the rough bark on the trunk. On the other hand, you might use long, smooth brush strokes to get the feeling of a long, straight branch, and brief, curly brush strokes to suggest the leaves.

The textures shown above are just a few of the obvious possibilities. Take a sheet of paper and see how great a variety you can discover for yourself. Try applying the paint in thick, lumpy gobs. Try thin, watery washes. Use your brush in different ways, and then see what other tools you can utilize, such as sticks, your fingers, a comb. You might even take a leaf, or a piece of corrugated board, or any rough material—paint it, then press it down on your paper to transfer its texture.

A Color Mosaic

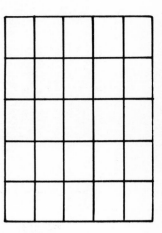

If you want to carry some of the experiments you've done a step further—and perhaps end up with a rather handsome design—paint a color mosaic. Take a sheet of paper no smaller than 11 by 14 inches, and rule it into rectangles as illustrated in the margin. Start by filling in one of the center spaces with a color—any color. Then mix a color that will look interesting next to it. If you started with a blue, for example, you might want to try a purple next to it. Then choose a color to go above the blue. Would you want a warm color in contrast? Or perhaps a less intense color, such as a grey-green to set off the blue? As you proceed to fill in the spaces, try all kinds of combinations—light against dark, gentle colors next to vivid ones, colors that harmonize, others that clash and fight.

You'll have to make a great many decisions by the time all the spaces are filled. And that is exactly the purpose of these color experiments—to get you to *think* about the colors you are using, rather than to choose arbitrarily or accidentally whatever is closest at hand.

There is no correct or incorrect way to make a painting like this. It is an exercise to enable you to see how various colors work in relation to one another. Every person will have his own ideas about color combinations.

Some modern artists get so involved with the problems and the language of color that they paint pictures using no more than two or three or four colors. But these colors are chosen and mixed with infinite care, and the relationship of one to another is given a great deal of thought.

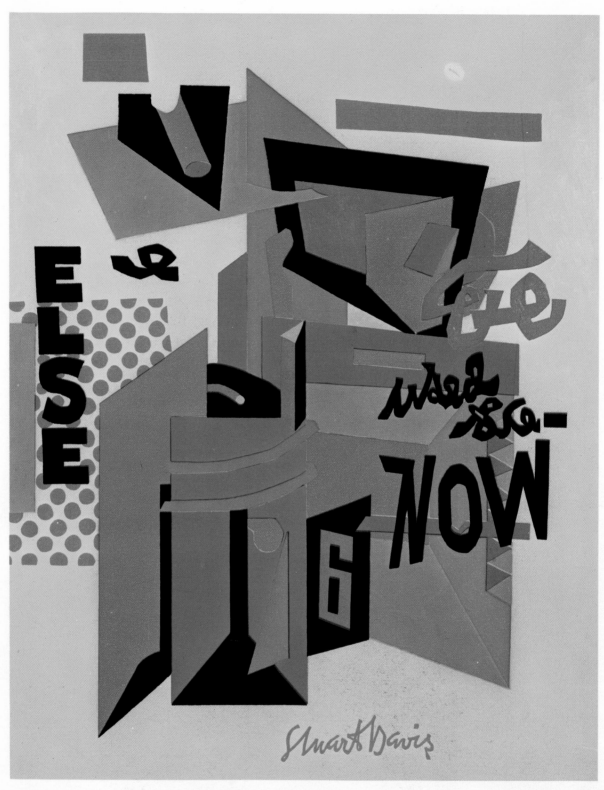

OWH! IN SAN PAO, *Stuart Davis, Whitney Museum of American Art*

Shapes And Forms

Just as pure color can suggest mood and feeling, so can shapes and forms. And just as there are exciting or monotonous colors, there are exciting or monotonous forms. The painting on the facing page, by Stuart Davis, is concerned simply with color and shape. The colors are very strong and the shapes have a vigorous, shifting movement. The words and letters that appear in the painting are used not for their meaning, but for the sake of their form and pattern. The painting has a quality of nervous excitement. Here is an example where color and form, without realistic subject matter, suggest a definite mood and feeling.

At the bottom of this page are four different forms. (They are shown in black, so that color won't influence their mood.) Can you see that each form has a different character? What is the mood of the shape on the left? Busy nervousness, perhaps? Does the shape to the right of it suggest strength and power? What about the others?

Two little paintings of a harbor scene are illustrated below. In both paintings you have the same elements: boats, clouds, hills, docks, reflections. Yet they are different. The difference lies in the kinds of shapes and forms that are used. In one painting the forms are nervous and jagged, giving an impression of activity and excitement. The other painting uses shapes which are rounder, softer, more gentle, suggesting a tranquil harbor.

Cut out some paper shapes and try a few experiments. Begin with three rectangles, and try them in different positions. You'll find that even when the shapes are identical, some arrangements are more interesting than others, as illustrated below.

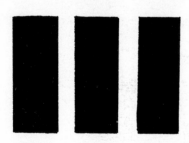 

These three rectangles, one next to the other, make a rather dull, monotonous group.

These two arrangements are much more interesting to look at.

After you've exhausted the possibilities of the rectangle, cut out three *different* shapes—such as an oval, a square, and a rectangle. With dissimilar shapes like these you have many more possibilities. See if you can make some groupings of these shapes that look especially interesting.

16

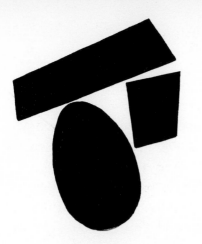

You'll find that the most successful arrangements have various contrasts and harmonies of size, contour, and shape. For example, the arrangement in the illustration on the left above is pleasing because of the contrast of the two sharp-edge rectangles with the smooth, round center shape. The arrangement to the right of it is interesting because of the relationship of the large, wavy shape with the three small, square shapes.

These kinds of form and shape relationships are quite subtle, and often difficult to explain. Sometimes shape relationships are interesting because there is a contrast between elements. Sometimes there is an interest that exists because of a similarity, or a rhythm, or a repetition, or an evolution, or a balance, or a tension. Sometimes you just intuitively *know* that certain shape combinations look well — just as sometimes you can't really explain, although you know, that certain color combinations succeed, others don't.

MAHONING, *Franz Kline, Whitney Museum of American Art*

Shapes And Color

It is, of course, possible to use shapes without color. Sculptors certainly do this. Most etchings, lithographs, and drawings are made without color, and there are even some painters who limit themselves to black and white. The very dramatic painting by Franz Kline, a modern American painter, illustrated at the bottom of the previous page, uses only black paint on white canvas.

However, form *and* color are the ingredients from which most paintings are made. Some artists find the possibilities and challenges of pure form and color so interesting they concern themselves with nothing else. They aren't in the least interested in painting trees, or people, or other recognizable objects.

Now that you've made a few experiments with combinations of shapes, as described on the previous two pages, let's go a little further and use shapes of different colors. If you have colored papers you can use them, otherwise use your paints. (If you are using paints, first draw your shapes lightly with pencil, then color them in.)

The trick now is to use colors that have the mood and feeling of the shapes. If, for example, you make a combination of nervous shapes, see if you can mix some nervous colors. If you have fat, lazy shapes, try to find colors that have that feeling.

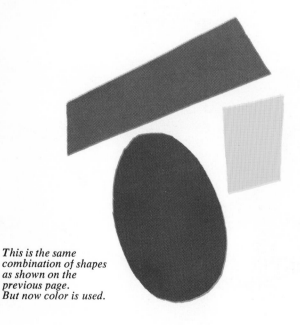

This is the same combination of shapes as shown on the previous page. But now color is used.

The illustrations on these pages show colors that have the same feeling as the shapes. (However, your paintings should express different ideas and use altogether different colors.) The combination of shapes on the left looks solid and sedate, and the colors have the same quality. The odd-looking fellow above is painted with rather odd colors. And the "floating checkerboard" below uses—yes, "floating" colors!

Finding Shapes

Here is an interesting way to experiment with some shape and color designs: take a sheet of heavy paper and with scissors cut out a not-too-complicated form. Place this on top of another piece of paper and lightly trace its outline with a pencil. Then move this cut-out form somewhere else on the paper and outline it again. Let it overlap the first outline. Do this several times.

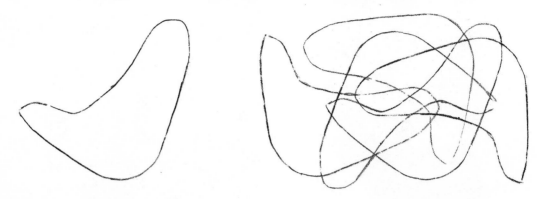

You have now a lightly penciled drawing which will contain a great tangle of shapes. Get your colors and fill in the shapes that you find most interesting. Don't hesitate to change or go beyond the pencil markings. The purpose of the pencil lines is simply to suggest different forms to you and get you started. Think about the colors you are using, and remember some of the color experiments from the previous pages.

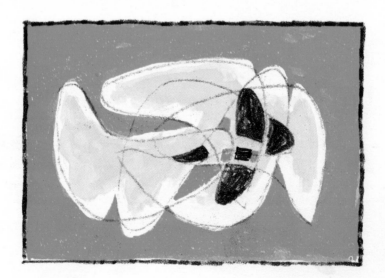

There are shapes everywhere about us, wherever you look. There are even shapes where no shapes exist! That sounds like double talk, but it isn't, because a shape can be formed in space *between* various objects. The space between the two vases illustrated below has a shape—the shape of a circle. Shapes of

this kind are called negative shapes. It is the shape "left over" from a positive shape. In the drawing below, the shape of the hills is important in the design, but equally important is the shape of the sky. They are *both* shapes, though the sky shape is the "left over" one.

 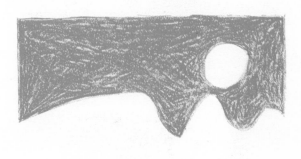

As you work on paintings or drawings, or for that matter any design problem (such as making a wallpaper, or deciding on a decorating scheme for a room, or designing a dress) judgments about color and form are continually taking place in your mind —sometimes consciously, sometimes subconsciously. And the ability to make these judgments is a basic part of your artistic effort.

Light And Shadow

There is an expression about an object being as visible as a black cat on a coal pile in a black cellar at midnight. However, that cat could be yellow with purple dots, sitting on a bright green sofa, and he would still be unseen if there was no light at all in that cellar. The shape and form of solid objects is apparent only because of light and shadow.

Make a fist and hold it up in front of you. Then slowly turn and twist and tilt it one way and then another. You'll see the patterns of light and shadow change as you move your fist. Notice in the illustration below how different the cube appears in different lights. And see how the ball can appear as either a simple flat circle or a solid heavy object, depending on where the light comes from.

If you want to indicate solidity and volume in your paintings, you must be aware of light and shadow. When and if you do use shadows in your paintings, don't just mix a batch of black and drop it in where you think a shadow belongs. A shadow area, like our cat in the cellar, is simply an area of

22

PAINTING, 1953, *Joan Miro, The Solomon R. Guggenheim Museum*

color with little light on it. The shadow (unless there is abso-
lutely no light) will be of a definite color. It may be a blue
or purple or brown, or even red, but it is rarely a solid black.

Many modern painters don't concern themselves with shadow, because they are not interested in creating an illusion of
solidity. They know that the paper or canvas upon which they
work is flat, and they accept the fact that they can't create a
three-dimensional object. (That's the work of a sculptor.) They
are more concerned with the use of color and shape. The painting by Joan Miro, reproduced above, is an example of a picture
that ignores realistic, modeled form in favor of abstract form.

What Are Paints?

The color in paints comes from pigments. A pigment is a substance that imparts a color to another material. Some pigments are found in the earth, some in plants or roots, some are manufactured chemically. During the time of the Renaissance one pigment was actually ground up from a semiprecious blue stone called lapis lazuli. As you can imagine, this was a very expensive color and used sparingly.

Yellow ochre pigment, for example, is a form of iron oxide. And this identical pigment is used to make yellow ochre oil paint, yellow ochre water color, yellow ochre pastels, yellow ochre poster paints, and so on. The "vehicle" or material with which the pigment is mixed is what gives the paint its particular character. When the pigment is mixed with an oil vehicle, such as linseed oil, you have oil paints. When the pigment is mixed with water you get water color. In pastels there is no vehicle. The pigment is just held together in stick form by means of a glue.

As an experiment you might try making some of your own colors. If you can find some red-brown soil, take a handful of it, grind it to a fine powder and mix it with some linseed oil and you have a brown paint. See what happens if you grind up some yellow autumn leaves, coffee, blueberries, or rust and mix them with linseed oil or glue or water. There is even one kind of paint that consists of pigments mixed with egg white. It is called egg tempera.

You can use a spoon and bowl for grinding colors.

Since color is such an important part of painting, you might find it interesting to know a little about color from a scientific point of view. Basically, color is a form of radiated energy! Just as a radio transmitter radiates energy in the form of radio waves, the sun (or an artificial light source) radiates energy in the form of light rays.

And just as radio stations can operate on many different frequencies (which you locate by tuning your radio dial), light is composed of many frequencies which we call colors, and which we can also "tune in."

Let us suppose a ray of sunlight (which appears white, but which contains all colors) shines on a piece of paper. If the nature of this piece of paper is such that it absorbs all the color frequencies in the sunlight except red, the paper will appear red. The red part of the beam of light has struck the paper and been reflected back to our eye. All the other colors contained in the beam of light have been absorbed by the paper and we do not see them. When you brush paint on paper, what you are doing in effect is spreading a *layer* of material on the paper that will absorb some color frequencies and reflect others.

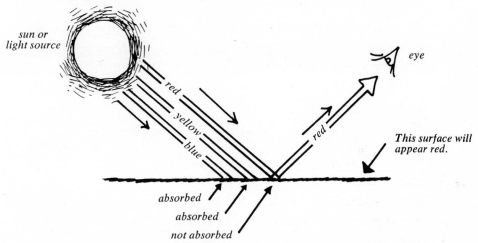

The reason some color frequencies are absorbed and others are reflected is quite technical and involves the molecular structure of the materials themselves. The study of color and light is called optics. It is extremely fascinating, but it is much too involved and scientific to go into in any detail in this book. If you want to learn more about this field, look in your library for some books on light and optics.

All colors are contained in sunlight. This can be demonstrated by shining a ray of sunlight through a prism. The prism will separate the white light into its component colors as illustrated here.

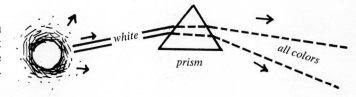

PART TWO   How To Paint

The Obvious – And Beyond

In painting—and in all art—there are many ways of saying the same thing. And just as it isn't very wise accidentally to use the first color that comes to hand when painting, it is also not very wise to take the first obvious idea that comes to mind.

Suppose you decided to paint an apple. Your first thought might be something like the drawing in the margin. But an apple is more than this: An apple is seeds, and skin, and color and texture. An apple is eaten. It is sliced. It is peeled. It is something that grows on a tree. It can be red or green or yellow or speckled. It can throw a shadow.

These imaginative extensions and explorations by the artist are what make a painting interesting and exciting. A totally realistic rendition of the object will rarely do this.

When you are working on your own paintings — whether figures or heads or landscapes—try to go beyond the obvious. Ask yourself what *you,* the artist, have to say about it.

I AND THE VILLAGE, *Marc Chagall, The Museum of Modern Art, New York. Here is an example of the artist extending the reality of a scene. An obvious painting of this subject might show a village street or some peasants working. But how mysterious and magical the picture becomes when the artist's memories and images are combined and altered and overlapped in this fantastic manner.*

The Shape Of The Figure

The human figure has been drawn, modeled and painted more than any other subject. Artists always find it varied, interesting, expressive, and challenging. Once you understand the basic structure and proportions of the human body, it is not difficult to paint. Think of the figure as a group or combination of oval shapes, as shown below. The head is an egg-shaped oval. The chest is another quite large oval. So are the hips. The arms, legs, hands, and feet can also be simplified into longer oval shapes.

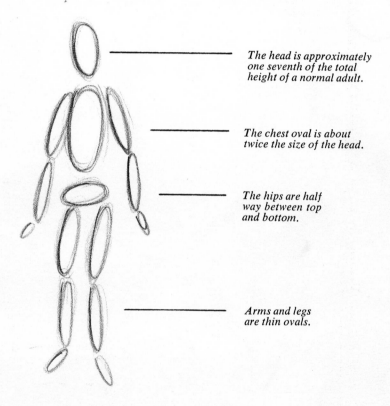

The head is approximately one seventh of the total height of a normal adult.

The chest oval is about twice the size of the head.

The hips are half way between top and bottom.

Arms and legs are thin ovals.

The way these shapes are placed in relation to one another will indicate almost any possible position of the human figure.

Mix up a batch of thin, very diluted poster paint—any color, but not so intense that it will be distracting. Tan is good. Now practice painting a few oval figures. Make them simply standing with hands at their sides. Try to get a sense of the proportions of all the parts. Don't, for example, make the head oval as large as the chest oval. Notice that the hip oval is horizontal, and that the arm and leg ovals are quite thin.

When you're able to get the ovals placed and proportioned so that they look like a human figure, then start to shift the ovals around to suggest some action. Tilt the chest oval. Bend the arms and legs. Make at least a dozen oval figures in all kinds of positions—running, bending, jumping, and so on.

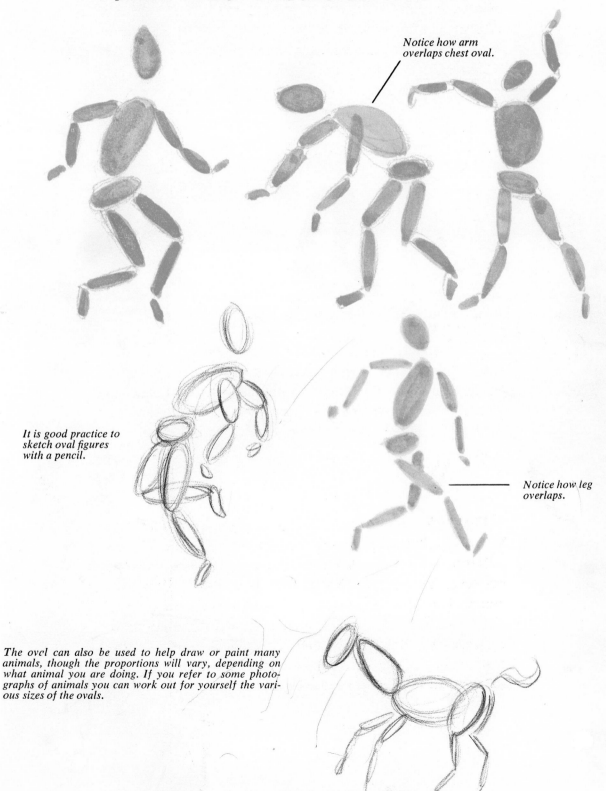

Notice how arm overlaps chest oval.

It is good practice to sketch oval figures with a pencil.

Notice how leg overlaps.

The oval can also be used to help draw or paint many animals, though the proportions will vary, depending on what animal you are doing. If you refer to some photographs of animals you can work out for yourself the various sizes of the ovals.

Painting The Figure

Now make some more oval figures, and when you are satisfied with the way they look, let the paint dry, then paint *over* the ovals with your paints mixed to a normal thickness. The ovals will be not visible any more. They have served their purpose by helping you assemble a correctly proportioned figure.

As you apply your opaque color over the ovals, think about the clothing you want your figures to wear. And you might find it fun to use something more exotic than the usual pants and shirts, or skirts and blouses. What about a knight in armor, a queen in a regal gown, a tramp, or a clown? What else can you think of?

This is the oval arrangement of the postman in Van Gogh's painting on the opposite page.

POSTMAN ROULIN, *Vincent van Gogh, Museum of Fine Arts, Boston*

As you use your color, try to remember some of the color experiments you did. Don't use the primary colors right out of the jar—unless you know you want obvious, strong color. If you were painting a clown this might be suitable. But if you are painting an elegant lady in an evening dress, you will prefer a more subdued or elegant color. Costume and fashion designers often make little figure paintings like these when they are planning a stage or movie production or trying out new fashion ideas.

If you want to expand your figure paintings, do something with the background. You might fill in a solid color, or you could paint in some background material. If you have painted a knight in armor, for example, you might want to paint a castle in the background, or some banners or tents.

After you've read about some of the other art media described in this book, such as oil paints or water colors or pastels, you will probably want to try doing some more figure paintings using these other materials. Remember the basic shapes and proportions of the figure, and you will have no difficulty.

SPRING FESTIVAL ON THE RIVER, *Chinese, Ming Dynasty (1368-1644), The Metropolitan Museum of Art. Chinese artists often made paintings on long strips of paper or silk. These paintings were rolled up and viewed a section at a time. This illustration is one part of a scroll 11¾ inches high and 33 feet long! The innumerable little figures are combined with the landscape to give a pretty clear idea of what this festival must have been like.*

MOTHER AND CHILD, *Pablo Picasso, The Art Institute of Chicago. In this painting the two figures have been greatly simplified. Picasso wanted to get a feeling of heavy, massive solidity. Picasso is generally considered to be the most important artist of our time. He has worked in many different styles, ranging from the realistic to the completely abstract. This painting is from his "classical" period.*

STARRY NIGHT, *Vincent van Gogh, The Museum of Modern Art, New York*

Oil Paints

The great majority of paintings you see in museums and galleries are done in oils. Most artists consider oil paints their basic medium. There are several reasons why this kind of paint is so popular.

Probably its greatest attraction is that it is so responsive. It will do almost anything you want it to do. It can be slapped on in great violent slashes with a large brush. It can be troweled on with a palette knife. The paint can be applied in thick, heavy gobs; it can even be squeezed right out of the tube onto the canvas—like toothpaste!

On the other hand, oil paints can be thinned with turpentine almost to the consistency of water, and the colors delicately built up layer over layer. The finest details can be painstakingly painted with a tiny brush. And because oil paints dry slowly (it takes a day or two for them to dry) one color can be blended into another.

It is also easy to make changes with oil paints. Before the paint dries, you can scrape off anything you don't want with a palette knife and try again.

The painting by Vincent van Gogh on the opposite page is an example of a painting done in a bold, vigorous style. The paint was applied in thick, firm strokes, and every stroke of the brush is apparent. The colors, too, are bold and strong. The painting by Claude Monet, on Page 2, is another example of a picture where the paints are applied heavily. This painting seems almost radiant with light and color.

In both of these paintings it is not hard to imagine the artists working with feverish enthusiasm, rushing to get a vision out of their minds and onto the canvas. There is quite a difference between violent, exciting brushwork like this, and the calm, controlled painting of the Ghirlandaio portrait on Page 51, or the precisely designed areas of the Stuart Davis painting on Page 14. Yet, oil paints are suitable for either of these ways of working.

Materials For Oil Painting

Oil paints are sold in tubes and come in various grades ranging from cheap to very expensive. The cheap colors are so diluted that a lot of cheap color is apt to go no further than a small amount of good color. The medium-priced colors are recommended.

A good basic assortment of colors to start with is: cadmium yellow medium (the "cadmium" refers to the chemical pigments used in the colors, and "medium" refers to the intensity), ultramarine blue, cadmium red medium, burnt sienna (this is a dark brown), black, viridian green, and a large tube of titanium white. You can mix just about any color you will need from these seven, but eventually you will probably want to buy some additional colors so that you won't have to do so much mixing. Some useful additional colors are: yellow ochre, alizarin crimson, cobalt blue.

You'll also need a bottle of turpentine. Turpentine is mixed with the paints to thin them, and is used to clean your brushes. A small bottle of linseed oil is also needed. It is mixed with the paints along with turpentine if you want to make the colors more transparent or give them a more oily texture. In addition, you'll need two small jars or tins in which to keep the turpentine and linseed oil while you are using them.

A piece of glass placed on top of a sheet of white paper will make a fine palette on which the paints can be mixed. Oil-paint brushes are different from the kind used for poster paints or water colors. (Though you could use them if you had nothing else.) Oil-paint brushes are flat and somewhat stiff. You should have three sizes: #2, #5, and a large #8. A palette knife is essential for handling the paints on your palette, for cleaning up the palette, and sometimes for mixing colors. It can also be used to scrape paint off the canvas. You also need some rags.

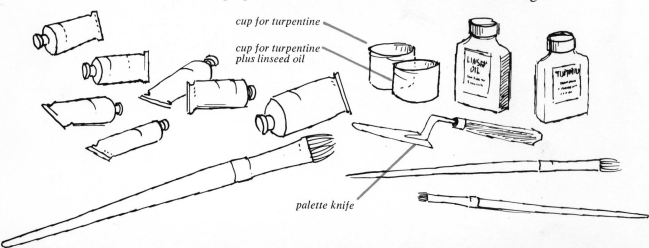

cup for turpentine

cup for turpentine plus linseed oil

palette knife

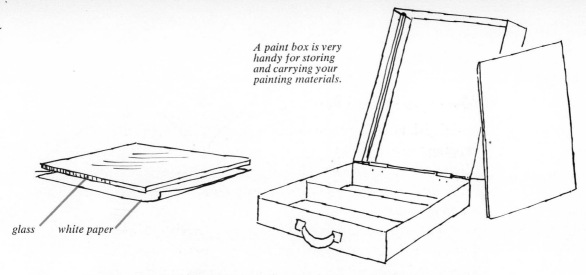

A paint box is very handy for storing and carrying your painting materials.

glass   white paper

Cotton or linen canvas, stretched over a wooden frame, is used by most experienced painters, but for your early efforts get the less expensive canvas board. This is a piece of canvas glued onto a heavy cardboard, and is available in a great many sizes.

There is one big difficulty with oil paints—they are hard to clean up. If you get paint on your hands you'll have to wipe it off with a rag dipped in turpentine. Paint on your clothes is very hard to remove. Wear the oldest clothes you have and work where any dripped or spattered paint won't ruin a good rug or furniture. When you finish painting for the day, wash your brushes carefully with turpentine to remove any trace of paint. Then wash them in soap and water. If you don't clean your brushes, the paint will dry on the bristles and ruin them.

What To Paint

There are subjects for painting everywhere you look. Some subjects may seem so beautiful you will wonder how you can hope to reproduce their beauty in a picture. For example, you might one day see a flower-covered hilltop at sunset. How can you capture something like this with paint and canvas? Well, you can't! There is no paint that burns as hot as the sun, and no color that has the smell of thistle or bayberry at twilight. Nor is there a brush small enough to paint every blade of grass. But what the artist *can* do is to show how he feels about his subject. His reactions, emotions, and thoughts are the material for his painting. If you were painting a sunset, for example, how would you paint the sun? Would you simply paint a round,

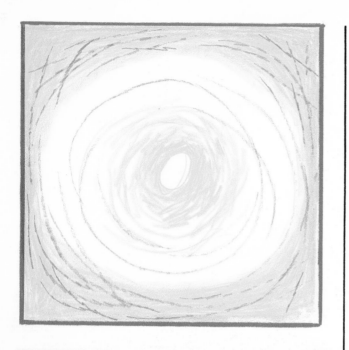

yellow disc? You might feel that the sun is a hole in the sky, a pattern of spreading circles, or a great fire. In the painting by Vincent van Gogh, a Dutch painter, reproduced on Page 34, the sky is filled with madly whirling spirals of many colors. These thoughts, experiences, and poetic visions can only come from the artist. The task of the artist is to interpret and extend the real world around him—not simply to record or copy what he sees.

How To Paint A Picture With Oil Paints

Let's use the photograph at the top of the page as a subject for painting. At first glance this scene probably looks like a hopeless jumble. It is crammed with a thousand details and cluttered with innumerable disorganized elements. You might think it is an impossible subject to reproduce. And it *is* impossible to reproduce exactly.

What you must do is use your intelligence and imagination to interpret this scene. You must select and use only those elements which you feel are most interesting to you, or most moving, or best suited for a dramatic composition. There are an almost infinite number of pictures which can be painted from this photograph.

A few of the possibilities are illustrated above. However, since this will be your first oil painting, it would be a good idea to use the possibilities contained in the sketch on the left. Since the photograph is, of course, black and white, you will have to decide what colors to use in your painting.

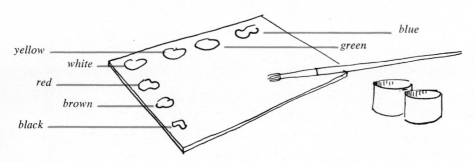

yellow
white
red
brown
black

blue
green

The paints are placed on the palette, as shown here.

Now prepare your palette. Squeeze out about a half-inch of each of your oil colors onto your palette. Pour a little turpentine into a small cup or jar. In another cup mix equal parts of turpentine and linseed oil. This mixture is called your "medium." Put your canvas board on an easel, or place it on a chair as shown. (Directions for making an easel are given on Page 63.)

With a pencil, very lightly indicate the various sections or color areas in your painting. One color area will be the building. The leaves on the tree will be another, and so on. A good deal of the confusion in the photograph we are working from is due to the rubble that is scattered about. Your painting can be greatly clarified if you paint the ground as a simple, uncluttered area.

Decide which color you want to use in each area. Then with a large brush, "tint" each area the color you want. A tint is simply a small amount of color mixed with a lot of turpentine. Tints can be brushed on rapidly over large areas, and will dry quickly. These thin washes of color provide a guide to your color scheme, and help to set the tone of the painting.

When all the tints have been painted on, you can begin to apply your color more heavily and carefully. Now add a drop or two of the medium (the turpentine and linseed oil mixture) as you mix the colors on your palette. This makes the paint more liquid or oily. How much you use will depend on your particular tastes and manner of working. You must clean your brush when changing from one color to another. Use the plain turpentine—not the medium—to do this.

The area of your painting occupied by the house is rather large, so you might want to start on that. The colors that you mix and apply now do not have to be the same as your original thin washes. They can, in fact, be entirely different. Sometimes the tint color, appearing through gaps and spaces in the second layer of a different color, is quite rich and interesting. This is a device that many painters use to make an area of color vibrant and alive. If, for example, you tinted your entire canvas a light green and then painted over that with other colors—letting little snatches of the green poke through—you would get something like the effect Joe Lasker got in his painting reproduced on Page 43.

The tree is another important element in this painting, and you can work on that next. Choose your color for the tree trunk carefully. Don't just mix up any old brown or black. And what color will you use for the foliage? There are a great many different kinds of green—though you don't have to use green at all!

As you continue to work on your painting, jump from one section to another. Don't complete the house, then the tree, then the fence, etc. Rather, do a little painting on the house, a little on the tree, a bit on something else, then come back to the house, and so on. This will help to keep the painting unified.

Sometimes colors can be mixed with the palette knife more easily than with the brush. Since the palette knife can be wiped clean very easily with a rag, it can be used to pick up fresh dabs of pure color from the paints along the sides of your palette. This will keep your pure colors from being contaminated by the colors you are in the process of mixing.

As your painting develops, you will certainly want to make changes. Perhaps one color will jar unpleasantly with another. Or maybe you don't like the shape or position of something. In that case, take your palette knife and carefully scrape away the offending area, and try again. In general, it is not a good idea to keep painting one layer of paint over another wet layer. The colors will blend together and get muddy. You can, of course, alter a color that is already on the canvas by adding another color to it and brushing it in.

THE BACKYARD, *Joe Lasker. This painting shows how a skilled, experienced artist used the material contained in the photograph reproduced on page 39. The painting has a great variety of warm colors—browns, greys, reds and soft greens. But this variety of color is all in the same family. The colors are warm, dark, subdued. There are no strong blues, yellows or whites. The bright, light green in the upper right, and the bright orange in the shirts, relieve and set off, what would otherwise be a too somber color scheme. You can also see that the many different elements in the painting have been placed and organized so that there is no clutter or confusion.*

As your painting progresses, you will want to give some thought to the textures in different areas. In the foliage of the tree you might want to use a small brush and apply the paint in rounded, swirling strokes. The ground might be painted with short dabs. Whatever you do, try to get a variety of textures.

43

When you are satisfied with the large areas, you can begin to work on some of the details. Use a smaller brush, and choose lively colors. For example, you might want to make the boy near the tree wear a bright yellow shirt. And the clothing on the line—here's an opportunity to introduce some bright, strong color.

Don't be discouraged if your painting doesn't please you, or seems to be turning out poorly. This happens to all artists and it happens very frequently. If it happens to you, stop working on the painting and put it aside. Perhaps when you look at it again an hour later, or two days later, you will see something that can be done to change it. If you really don't like the painting, simply scrape off all the paint with your palette knife, wipe the surface with turpentine on a rag, and start again. If the paint has dried on the canvas, cover the dried paint with a coat of white. The white paint will keep your first attempt from distracting you. When the white has dried you are ready to start again.

When you finish painting, dip your brushes in turpentine, dry them on a rag, then wash them with soap and water. Clean your palette by scraping off the leftover paint in the center. The pure colors on the sides of your palette will remain usable for a few days, so you can leave them if you intend to paint again within that time. Otherwise, scrape them off.

LANDSCAPE (detail),
attributed to Sheng Mou,
Chinese, Fifteenth Century,
The Art Institute of Chicago

The Rules Of Perspective

Perspective is the technique of getting drawn or painted objects to look as if they logically belonged in the space they occupy. There are five basic rules which are illustrated below.

Make some experimental drawings with pencil and paper and try out these rules for yourself. Once you understand them, you can make use of them in your drawings and paintings—or you may prefer to ignore them if they get in the way of what you want to do. The painting by Joan Miro illustrated on Page 23 pays little attention to any perspective rules.

1. Things look large when close, smaller as they get farther away.

2. Objects close by are brighter and more vivid than those in the distance. Distant objects look vague and hazy.

3. An object will overlap what is behind it.

4. As objects get farther away they usually appear higher up—as well as smaller.

5. Parallel lines appear to get closer to each other as they get farther away. They appear to touch at the horizon.

PORTRAIT OF THE ARTIST, *Rembrandt,*
The Metropolitan Museum of Art

ICHIKAWA KOMAZO II, *Toshusai Sharaku,*
The Metropolitan Museum of Art

BOY IN BLUE JACKET, *Amadeo Modigliani,*
The Solomon R. Guggenheim Museum

How To Paint A Head

Sooner or later you are going to want to try doing a portrait of someone. For your first attempt, use the most convenient model you can find—yourself. Do a self-portrait. Set up a large mirror next to your canvas. Then take some time to study the characteristics of your face. Are your eyes far apart? Is your nose short or long? Is there something distinctive about your hair, your complexion, your ears? If you can pick out and analyze the distinctive features of your head, it will be easier for you to get a likeness.

When you are ready to start, prepare your palette by squeezing out your colors. The directions given here are for oil paints, but you can follow the same procedure using any other kind of paints. Pour out a little turpentine into one container and linseed oil and turpentine (your medium) into another container. Begin by mixing up some color, very thinned out with turpentine. With a large brush, use this color to paint in the silhouette of your head. (A silhouette shape is an outline of a shape. It does not necessarily mean a profile of your head.)

Even though this head shape will show no features, it will have a lot to do with whether you get a likeness of yourself or not. The conventional shape of a head is an egg-like oval. But there are a great many variations. Some heads are perfectly round, others long and thin, others squarish.

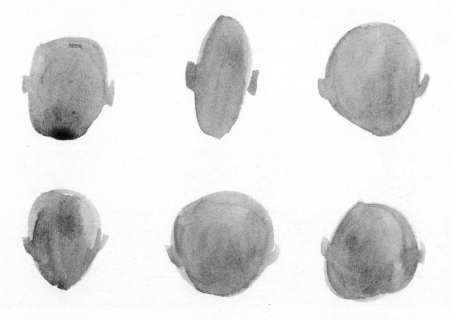

The typical face has its features distributed as shown in the drawings below. Most faces vary from these classical proportions, of course. And it is these variations that make for individuality.

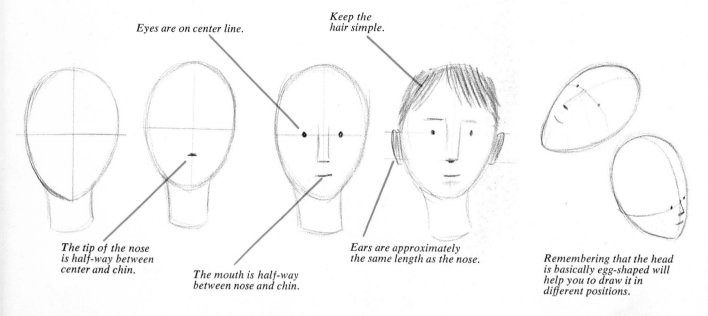

Eyes are on center line.

Keep the hair simple.

The tip of the nose is half-way between center and chin.

The mouth is half-way between nose and chin.

Ears are approximately the same length as the nose.

Remembering that the head is basically egg-shaped will help you to draw it in different positions.

Now you can begin on some of the features. The nose is a good landmark, and usually there is more light on it than the rest of the face because it projects and catches the light. There is often a little shadow under the tip, and sometimes along the side, depending on where the light is coming from. What is the color of the shadow?

Before you get too involved with the head itself, begin to paint the background. At this point, just put in some thinned-out color so that you will have something more than bare white canvas around the head. As you know from some of the color experiments in the beginning of the book, one color affects another. The background colors should relate in some way to the colors in the head itself. The background can be lighter, or darker, in contrast, or in close harmony with the colors of the head. Give it a little thought and perhaps refer to some of your earlier color experiments before you decide. Later, if you feel more ambitious, you may want to include some of the room around you, or even paint in a whole scene.

Now get back to your face. Skip about your painting as you work. Don't finish one section and then proceed to another. Rather, do some painting on the nose, go on to rough in the ears perhaps, or start the mouth, then move on elsewhere. This might seem a little haphazard, but what it does is to keep the entire painting balanced and unified.

As you work on your portrait, you will find that there is a surprising variety of color that you can use. You may find traces of red in some areas. The side of the face which receives less light may have a greenish tinge. Sometimes the shadows around the eyes may appear blue or purple.

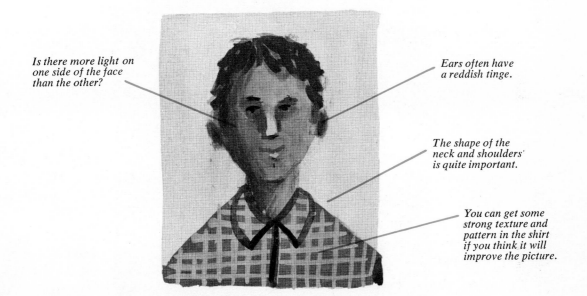

Is there more light on one side of the face than the other?

Ears often have a reddish tinge.

The shape of the neck and shoulders is quite important.

You can get some strong texture and pattern in the shirt if you think it will improve the picture.

When you paint the hair, try to get the main shapes rather than individual wisps or strands of hair. Don't get too fussy with little details. One or two strokes of your brush, if planned in advance, can suggest the eyes. One simple line (not necessarily black) can indicate the mouth, and you'll probably see that there is a small shadow under the lower lip. The lips themselves are rarely a bright red.

The eye is an oval shape.

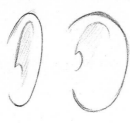

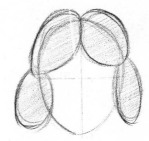

Girls' hair is more complicated and requires a little thought and planning before painting.

When you are almost finished, move back four or five paces and look through squinted eyes at what you've done. This will block out the details and will sometimes show you things which can be improved. Don't be too concerned if this first self-portrait doesn't turn out to look like you. If you have made a painting with good color and nice forms, that is accomplishment enough. If you keep trying, you will develop confidence and skill, and eventually you will be able to get a likeness of yourself or of other people.

LADY WITH A PINK (detail), Rembrandt, The Metropolitan Museum of Art. The painting and brushwork in this detail has a simple directness and assurance that is typical of Rembrandt.

A LADY OF THE SASSETTI FAMILY, *Domenico Ghirlandaio, The Metropolitan Museum of Art, The Michael Friedsam Collection. This portrait was made with tempera paint on wood, in the fifteenth century. It wasn't until the sixteenth century that oil paints came into common usage.*

51

Water Color

Water colors are thin, transparent paints that are mixed with water and applied to paper. They have a quality that is quite different from oil or poster paints. With one or two strokes of a large, loaded brush you can paint in a vivid sky. Another few strokes with a brown or a green and you can have a mountain, or a lake, and you will be well started on a water-color landscape. This quick, easy application of color gives water-color paintings a fresh and spontaneous look. It is one of the particular attractions of this kind of painting.

Materials: Water colors are sold in small tubes. A good beginning selection is: red, yellow, ultramarine blue, burnt sienna, viridian green, black. Do not get white. The white in a water-color painting is the color of the paper. Where you want white to appear you simply don't apply paint. If white is mixed with water-color paints the colors immediately become opaque and lose their sparkle. The colors then have the quality of poster paints.

Do not get the water-color sets which come in a small tin with the color contained in little square cakes. It is hard to get enough of a color on your brush.

You will also need several large dinner plates on which to mix your colors, and some brushes. Water-color brushes are soft and round. Use the brushes you used for poster paints: a small #3, a medium #6, plus a big #10 or #12. Two jars of water are needed—a large one to wash your brushes in, and one for the water you'll need to mix with the colors. You'll also need a drawing board.

The kind of paper you use is quite important. There is a variety of heavy, absorbent papers that are especially made for water-color painting. However, they are fairly expensive, and you can manage with any white paper that doesn't have a shiny surface, and that isn't too light and flimsy. The heavier the paper the better.

BAMBOO (detail), Chinese, attributed to Su Shih (1036-1101), The Metropolitan Museum of Art

Painting A Water Color

In order to see how water color differs from oil and tempera painting, let's try doing a landscape from the photograph above.

Your first task is to decide what you want to eliminate, because there is just too much to include everything. Illustrated below are some of the possibilities. One example concentrates on the texture of the foliage and pebbles in the foreground. Another concentrates on the old schooner. The painting on the right tries to make the most of the low hills in the background, the sheds, and fishing boats. Let's assume this latter arrangement is what you've decided to do. Your first step will be to draw *very lightly* with a pencil the position of these various elements. This will serve as a guide for your placement of color.

Begin by painting the water in the harbor. Squeeze out just a little touch of blue on the edge of one of your mixing plates. If you want to make a greenish-blue, you might also squeeze out a bit of yellow, or black. Now dip your brush—a big one—in water, and then into the blue, mixing it in the center of the plate. Add the yellow or black as you think necessary. Use plenty of water. When you are satisfied with the color, load the brush and sweep the color onto the paper with quick free strokes. While this is drying you can mix the color for the sky. After you paint the sky, paint the low scrubby hills in the background.

If you apply one wash of color over or adjoining another that is still wet, the colors will run together. This is sometimes extremely interesting, with soft, vague and subtle variations. If you don't want this to happen, let one color dry before adding another adjoining color.

This is a wash of color.

This is how a dab of color looks when applied to damp paper.

This is one color over another.

If you put tape or rubber cement on paper, apply paint, then remove the tape or cement, you get sharp, clean whites like this.

The paper will sometimes buckle slightly as you keep applying the water color, especially if you are using a lightweight paper. If this bothers you, let it dry and it will flatten out. Be sure not to paint right up to the edge of the paper, or the buckling will remain when the paper dries.

Now that you have painted the water and some of the background, you can start on the foreground and the shacks. As a general rule, paint your light colors first, your dark colors last. The reason for this is that water colors are transparent and it is impossible to make a dark area lighter unless you use white paint. And white paint will destroy the transparency and brightness that is characteristic of water color.

The value (lightness or darkness) of the color you mix can be altered by the amount of water you use with the pigment. For example, if you used a red with very little water added, it would be strong and dark. But if you added a good deal of water to the red, it would become light, and even pinkish.

When the main areas of your painting are in place, let the paper dry. Then you can paint some of the smaller, more detailed elements. Use a smaller brush, and as you choose and mix your colors, think back to some of the color experiments you made at the beginning of this book—and don't use black simply because the photograph shows black!

As you work you may find that there is too much paint in one place. You can blot it up with a dry brush, a sponge, or a piece of facial tissue.

56

The foreground in our photograph looks a little barren, and you might want to enlarge some of the foliage that appears in the left-hand corner. You might also want to add some of the small rowboats and lobster pots which can be seen piled up alongside the sheds.

There are as many different ways of using water colors as there are artists. Water colors can be used meticulously and with great detail, or on the other hand, it is possible to paint on paper that has been dampened all over, so that colors run and blend one into another. You might also find it interesting to combine pen and ink with water color. The relationship between loose, free color washes and the sharp, crisp pen-and-ink line can be very dramatic. Do a pen-and-ink drawing first, using waterproof ink, and add the color over the drawing. Another time start with water color, then do your drawing after the colors are dry.

Because the materials for water-color painting are not too bulky and the paper dries rapidly, water colors are ideal for outdoor sketching. Your paints, brushes, and a few small dishes and jars will fit into a small box which is easy to take along when you go off for a picnic or a trip. You can tuck under your arm a water-color pad or a couple of pieces of paper tacked to a drawing board or some illustration board.

RED BALLET SKIRTS, *Edgar Degas,*
Burrell Collection, Art Gallery and Museum, Glasgow, Scotland

Pastels

Pastels are sticks of pure, dry pigment. They are like colored chalks. Because neither oil nor water is mixed with the colors, pastel pictures have a very bright, crisp look about them.

But pastels have several drawbacks. Because the colors are chalky, they will smear or rub off when touched. You have to be rather careful and neat when you apply the pastels. Too much rubbing, blending, and fussing spoils the clear bright colors. In order to avoid this, most sets of pastels have a large variety of colors. When the picture is finished, it must be "fixed" by spraying the painting with some kind of protective coating.

The pastel by Edgar Degas, a French painter, which is illustrated on the opposite page, is an example of pastels used well. The colors are vivid and clear, and the typical chalky feeling of pastels is used to best advantage.

Materials: Pastels are available in any art store in sets of various sizes. The smaller sets will have about a dozen different colors, and the larger sets as many as forty or fifty colors. The larger the set the better.

Recently, there has been developed a kind of pastel which is called "oil color in stick form." These colors behave the same as pastels, but they are less chalky.

You also need fixative. This comes in a spray can or in a bottle. The bottled fixative is sprayed on by blowing through a little pipe arrangement as shown in the margin.

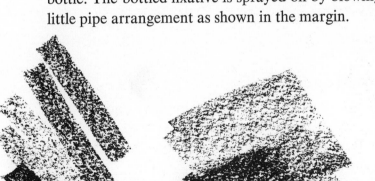

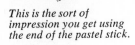

This is the sort of impression you get using the end of the pastel stick.

This is made with the side of a pastel stick.

This is made with a corner.

The best papers are pastel or charcoal papers. They come in many handsome colors as well as white. However, you can use almost any paper if it isn't smooth. Pastels won't apply easily onto a smooth or shiny surface.

There is no one specific way in which pastels should be applied. You'll have to experiment with them and decide for yourself what suits you best. One way of handling the pastels is to think of each mark you make on the paper as a brush stroke. In this way you can gradually construct your picture by means of individual strokes. This is a rather slow way of working, but it produces a very brilliant, shimmery sort of picture. The French Impressionists, who painted in the early 1900's and wanted to capture the pure color and vibrancy of what they saw, accomplished this by the use of oil colors applied in small dabs and not smoothed or blended one into the other. There are not many muddy browns or greys or blacks to be seen in the paintings of these artists. Even the dark shadows are full of color—greens and purples and lavenders. The painting by Renoir on Page 62 is a typical Impressionist painting.

If you are working for any length of time on a pastel picture, it is a good idea periodically to give it a light spray of fixative. This will help to keep the loose pigment from drifting about.

Because of the size and bluntness of the pastel stick and its softness, you will have trouble getting little details. This is one of the limitations of the material, and you will have to work accordingly.

Other Materials

In the last few years a new type of felt-tipped "painting pen" (sometimes called a "marker" pen) has become popular. The most common form is a small cylinder or bottle with a felt tip. These pens come in a great many intense colors. Because they leave a simple, bright, unchangeable mark they can be handled a little like pastels. You can't mix or blend a particular color because the ink dries almost instantly. You can only mix colors by putting one over another, or one right next to another.

The illustration on the next page was made with marker pens. As you can see there are no flat, even areas of color, and there

is no gentle smoothing of one tone into another. A solid tone is built up by means of a great many individual pen strokes.

Chemists have recently developed new plastics which are being used now in various kinds of paints. There are new poster paints which rapidly dry to a strong waterproof finish. This means that one layer of paint can be brushed over another without danger of the two mixing.

There are also new, plastic-based paints similiar to oil paints. These dry fast and adhere better than the conventional oil paints. They are mixed with water rather than turpentine or linseed oil.

After you have had some experience with the conventional paints described in this book, try some of these new materials. However, it doesn't really matter what is at the bristle end of your brush, but what is at the other end—your hand, your eye and your imagination.

IN THE MEADOW, *Auguste Renoir, The Metropolitan Museum of Art*

How To Make An Easel

An easel is a basic piece of equipment for any artist. This is particularly true if you use oil paints. It's quite a tricky task to balance a large canvas, thick with wet paint, on your knees, your desk, or a wobbly chair. The easel described here is quite simple and can be built with just a few hand tools. You can store it away by removing the cross-piece and loosening the bolt on top. When this bolt is loosened, the legs fold together and the whole thing can be tucked away in a corner of a closet.

You'll need the following materials:

Three pieces of 1-inch by 1-inch pine, each 6 feet long (with no cracks or knots).

Three pieces of 1-inch by 1½-inch pine, 2 feet long.

One ⅜-inch bolt, 4 inches long.

One ⅜-inch bolt, 5 inches long.

Four washers and two "butterfly" nuts for the bolts.

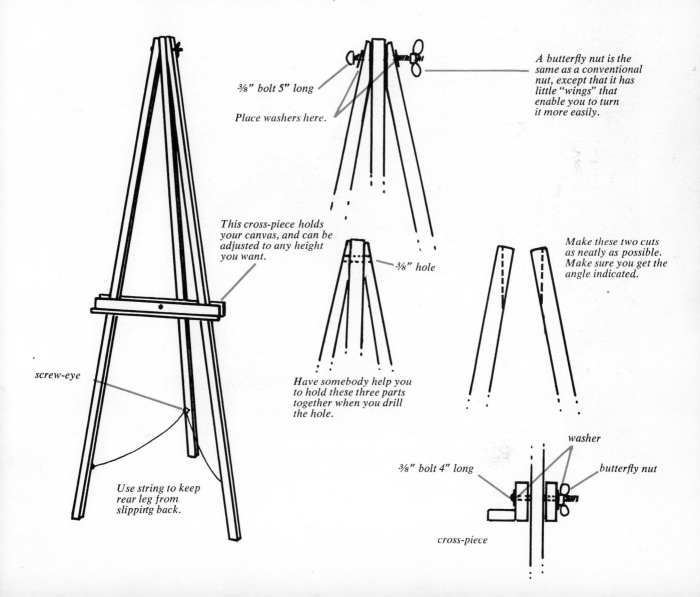

⅜" bolt 5" long

Place washers here.

A butterfly nut is the same as a conventional nut, except that it has little "wings" that enable you to turn it more easily.

This cross-piece holds your canvas, and can be adjusted to any height you want.

⅜" hole

Make these two cuts as neatly as possible. Make sure you get the angle indicated.

screw-eye

Have somebody help you to hold these three parts together when you drill the hole.

Use string to keep rear leg from slipping back.

⅜" bolt 4" long

washer

butterfly nut

cross-piece

Conclusion

This book has described some of the fundamental techniques of painting. It has tried to give you some feeling for color and form—how it can be used, what it can do. But in order for you to develop any real skill you must do more than read a book. For one thing, you should do a lot of drawing. Get yourself a sketch pad and draw people, scenes, still lifes—anything and everything at all, as often as you can. And you must also do a great deal of painting. Make yourself an easel like the one described on Page 63. Leave it standing with paper or canvas on it in a corner of your room. Then, when you get an idea or the urge to paint, you'll be ready to start work with a minimum of preparation. The more painting you do, the better artist you will be.

BE CAREFUL WITH THAT STEP, *Francisco Goya,*
The Art Institute of Chicago